CLOCKS
&
WATER DROPS

Marlene Hitt

CLOCKS
&
WATER DROPS

Marlene Hitt

Moonrise Press

Los Angeles 2015

Clocks and Water Drops by Marlene Hitt

This book is published by Moonrise Press
P.O. Box 4288, Los Angeles – Sunland
CA 91041-4288, www.moonrisepress.com
info@moonrisepress.com

The font Garamond is used throughout the text.

Manufactured in the United States of America

The Library of Congress Publication Data:

Hitt, Marlene, 1936–
[Poems. English]
Clocks and Water Drops / Marlene Hitt, author
118 pages (x pp. + 108 pp.) 15.2 cm x 22.9 cm. Written in English.
        Includes 73 poems, photos, and a portrait.
        ISBN 978-0-9819693-5-0 (paperback)
        I. Hitt, Marlene, 1936 – Poetry. II. Title.

10 9 8 7 6 5 4 3 2 1

PREFACE

During one of the Village Poets Monthly Readings at the Bolton Hall Museum in Tujunga, we started talking about great poetry. What are the themes for a good poem? What should the author write about? The grandiose subjects of saving the world from disaster and trauma, even trauma itself – war, suffering, death, rape, illness, depression, and cancer – are well represented in thousands of poetry books. There is a lot of anger out there at the way things are; there is a lot of sorrow that the state of the world is not, cannot, be better. Poetry is and should be the barometer of the times, the conscience of societies, the witness to our individual pains and tribulations.

Yet, too few poets write about their blessings, especially the beauty of the small things, Marlene Hitt said in our mini-discussion. Everyone is so angry, so dramatic. It seems much easier to catch the audiences' attention with shocking images of severed limbs, blood and guts, than by describing the strange feeling of gratitude for a seed caught in the teeth, gratitude for life itself. I could not agree more with this point of view. A couple of months later, I approached Marlene with a request to publish her next poetry book. It is a poet's mission, I think, to document the happiness and wistful melancholy of domestic life, to portray children running wild in the alleys, to capture the warmth of an afternoon in the kitchen, when a mother is teaching her daughter how to bake that perfect apple pie, spiced with cinnamon and love.

Marlene Hitt is an attentive poet, an inspired poet. She listens to the sounds of the past, disappearing from our electrified, virtually connected lives: the "plodding of beetles," the ticking of the grandfather clock, the tapp8ing of rain on the windowsill. She watches shifting hues in the sky and the mesmerized faces of children "glued" to their TVs; she sees how the children still brighten at the sight of the Christmas tree. Marlene shows her readers what a life well lived could be; she makes her poems from family stories, community celebrations and discoveries in the back alley. She portrays her grandparents and her children, yet she does not forget her neighbors, the homeless, the lost…

Clocks and Water Drops, her first full-length poetry collection, is a gift of "small things" – a gift of remembrance and affection, a whimsical and wise offering of carefully calibrated images and reflections. We are thankful for the talent of Marlene Hitt, the first Poet Laureate of Sunland-Tujunga, a historian of local communities, and a treasure of poetry in the Foothills.

Maja Trochimczyk, Ph.D.
President, Moonrise Press

CONTENTS

Preface by Maja Trochimczyk

Arrival — 2

CHILDREN — 3
Treasure — 4
First Grade — 5
Falling —7
Door Marked Boy/Girl — 8
Reunion — 9
Late Phone Calls — 10
Threaded Thoughts — 12
The First Time I Cried — 14
I Could Tell You About — 15
Curiosity — 16
Television — 17
Night Lights — 18

PORTRAITS — 19
Pages — 20
Lessons — 21
Women's Wear — 22
Cycles — 23
Well, then and how was *your* day? — 24
A Found Poem: The Lists — 25
A Song of Myself — 26
Tell Me a Story —27
I Could Tell You — 29

MARRIAGES — 31
Mates for Life — 32
Old Marriage I — 33
Old Marriage II — 34

Old Marriage III — 35
Old Marriage IV — 36
Old Marriage V — 37
Love Mended — 38

NEIGHBORS — 39
The Migrant — 40
Day Laborer — 42
I Wonder if I Will Ever See John Again — 43
Dead Man — 44
Jury Duty — 46
Mother — 48
Pity Party — 49
Pen Pals — 50

SEASONS — 51
Everywhere — 52
A Tale to Tell — 55
Mother's Day — 56
Easter Sunday — 57
No Grapes This Year — 58
Autumn, 1950 — 59
Station Fire — 61
Wild Fire — 62
What Would This Mean? — 63
A Terrible Awful No Darn Good Day? — 64
What Am I Thankful For? — 65
Slippingsliding — 67

SMALL THINGS — 69
Work of the Hands — 70
Three of Hearts — 71
Spring Cleaning — 72
The Decorator from Penny's — 73
Right and Wrong — 74

Photograph — 75
Broken… — 76
All That I Am — 77
Silence — 78
The Small Things — 79

Passages — 81
    Time — 82
    Time Capsule from 1914 — 83
    West of Hillrose — 84
    Take Me — 87
    The Alley — 88
    I Can Hear the Plodding of Beetles — 89
    The Remembering — 90

Farewells — 93
    Fields of My Childhood — 94
    The Old Clock — 95
    This Letter — 96
    The Estate — 98
    Memories — 100
    This Epitaph — 101
    Bury Me — 103

About the Author — 107

CLOCKS
&
WATER DROPS

Arrival

Please, come home.
Walk into the door of the kitchen
where stew and wheaten bread
steam, where a fire warms.
Your father will tune the strings,
unwrap the bohdran.
I will uncover the harp.
The stew will simmer.
With hands wiped on my apron
I will open my arms
to you, my firstborn child
so long traveling. Your sisters
will dance. The old ones will smile
through brown, gapped teeth,
will smile blue into your eyes.
Wrapped around you, the old songs,
the scent of turf fire, the smell
of our own wool and you will sing.
While you sleep
I will wrap around you a woven shawl
to shield you. Please come home
to bleating lambs,
to the resting place of love.

CHILDREN

Treasure

Here it is once again, way back in the closet,
the box of treasures collected by children.
Feathers, one huge and black from a crow,
one tiny from Felicia the finch.
And stones:
My mother's rock from the quarry
that inspired a song "Rock of Ages,"
New Zealand jade, a rounded pebble
from the Dead Sea.
This is where my penny went,
the one I wore in my shoe at our wedding
and the cigar, still wrapped, from when our son was born.
Keys, shaped for castle doors, for valises,
for piggy banks and diaries. Keys lost,
found far too late for any locks.
I remember the dandelions blown in the wind
and this one glued to a paper plate, imprisoned,
never to blossom and this Saskatchewan wheat
pulled up by Uncle Alf when he stopped the truck
to find a souvenir that last evening.
And this one magnificent marble!
What is not a treasure?
What can be tossed away?

First Grade

While her face was fat and round with childhood,
she held his hand, a blond-haired boy.
He gave her love, she gave it back
        with all the fire in her soul.

They picked grapes, hunted for coyote dens,
climbed the hills, walked dusty roads,
munched wild onions, breathed their scent.
One cold Monday morning
in the dark hallway at home
she sat alone and cried. After such sweet love,
        after the thinning of her fragile skin, after exposing

all her bones and nerves, she was cut deep with pain.
He told her on Saturday how much he loved her.
On Sunday he said his love was gone,
even as he handed her his last gift,
        the acorn necklace he had made.

She saw the hard distance in his eyes,
knew she could no longer find him there:
not in the fields, nor the meadows,
        nor the coyote runs. Wild onions lost their flavor,
        grapes their sweetness.
        In the dark hallway the child sobbed

until her love became vapor on the walls and rugs.
She was old. She was new.

On Monday, wearing a red sweater,
carrying a lunch box with rust on the hinges,
the child-woman felt absent. The classroom felt empty,
She thought she was not there. Blank pages filled her books,
silent words came from mouths that only seemed to speak.

Food did not fill her. A dream that was life
        seemed bad. She feared waking.

On Friday, she touched a peach from the peach tree.
She felt the fuzz on her lips.
She took a bite. It tasted good. It tasted real.
She looked for a grape from the vineyard
        and a wild onion. She thought she saw a coyote den.

She had almost forgotten him,
the blond-haired boy.

Falling

Graceful weeds flowed in the breeze,
wild oats had turned gold.
Mustard clothed in yellow blazed out
from that morning made of mist.
As drops of dew on your hair melted,
your brown curls turned black.

That day, so long ago, those dew drops
caught the morning sun, then vanished
into the summer heat, into dust on the road,
summer dust raised from our wheels
as we pedaled as fast as we could go.

One day, when you fell from the oak
you'd climbed to taunt me, to show
spindly manhood, I rushed to save you,
brushed leaves from your shirt, kissed you
full on your cheek. You hit me because
I was a girl! And you were a boy!
And boys don't kiss!

A decade later, I fell, you caught me,
said that I swooped to the floor with grace.
Always you stayed stronger, my brother,
I, the sister brat, always I loved you.
This Sunday we will meet again,
in a sunset that drips with rain.

Door Marked Girl/Boy,
Room Remodeled

On the wallpaper, bunches of roses.
Silk flowers stretch in a tall vase.
New floor, new, all new.
Walls fade and disappear
morph into the room that once was;
a small pedestal basin, off-white,
a toilet, a mirror, no more,
functional, a sticking door
open to my father's office,
another into grandpa's sitting room
where my baby lay sleeping
at his great-grandfather's feet
not minding the sound of
my father's adding machine
as it wheezed whick-whack
to the pull of his arm.
He added the totals of the bills.
In time the adding was done,
my shopping finished.
The child, the old, old man,
bald heads wanting my kiss,
small sculptures formed by a gentle
sculptor god. As I stand,
looking once more,
these new walls form to present tense,
into bunches of roses. Old doors are gone.
The new door opens easily,
the door of memory closes.

Reunion

My friend, do you remember
when you brought poppies
to my little table
when we were five?
When we made rose petal salads
and guava tea?
Do you remember
when you held my hand
that day when I needed you,
you whom I loved?
We meet again
kissing kisses that miss.
Your smile
now smiles too large.
You listen to my laugh
which laughs too long.
We speak of our old love
but fear the word that time
has changed.
At this linened table
we lunch on arugula and prawns,
starving for all that is lost.
Yet I am filled,
for I thought I would never
see you again,
and that is the reason
for all these tears.
Come back, rose petals,
guava tea. Come back
pure love of children.

Late Phone Calls

I.
It is late at night, early morning.
The telephone rings,
a question whispers,
"Do you know where your daughter is?"

Then comes the frantic leap
from our bed to hers.
She sleeps like a toddler,
knees drawn up, head tucked down,
She never is late for curfew.

Why does that question
cause such panic?
It is from not knowing
what might come next.

II.
Again, the phone rings
in the afternoon.
"Do as we tell you," the voice rasped
"or we will shoot your mother.
We mean it – a gun is pointed
at her head right now."

Mom! Oh Mom!
An old lesson returned
to her mind. Mom told us
"Save yourselves whenever you can,
then I can fight for myself."

She jumped into her brand new
stick shift sedan, screamed downhill
crashed into a eucalyptus.

The tree will die not long after.
The shiny white auto is totaled,
knees shattered, liver lacerated,
nose crushed.

The neighbor boys run out
hopping up and down
and laughing. A joke on the big sister
of the boy next door.
They were the only ones who laugh.

The firemen tug and pull,
medics measure vital signs.
Stitches are stitched, bones
rebuilt, liver sutured.
The family waits in the ICU.

It must have been worth the show.

Threaded Thoughts

Around this hand I wind
a yellow quilting thread
thick and strong
over and over, back onto itself.
Around my hand goes
the Bad Man thread;
with scissors I cut him out.
Mr. Barker's store
where I stole a ring,
I tie in a knot.
Tommy, whose thread
had snapped, whose death
changed the world.
Through my heart
winds a thread around kindness
and a doll from a stranger, one with
eyes that close and real hair.
Around and around I wind
the men in the drug store
who teased this child,
I tie them tight, choking them
below their lidded eyes.
Around and around their
smoke rings, cigarette burns
on the tables, smoke
blown into the eyes
of little girls sent to buy
"Wings, two packs for a quarter"
as they clutched their father's coin
or ration stamps from their mothers
who yearned for sugar, butter.
Around my hand, thread,
thick like a tumorous growth,

thread so many-colored
as to turn brown with the winding
into the brown of your eyes,
you, who saved me from one world
to place me into another
where we dragged ourselves
dreaming about bright kingdoms
and robes of kings.
One fine day the needle, threaded,
pierced my flesh. I bled
easily and long, spilled red
onto the thread around my hand,
the honest cotton through my heart
and around my arms.

With the threads knotted
and frayed I stitch my words
for you to see.

The First Time I Cried

is obvious, and all the people
ahhhed and ooohed.
I cried for this, for that,
and, because I could.
When "no's" came
and a little brother
and spanks and scrapes
I cried, bawled, sobbed,
hiccupped, threw up.
Tears streamed out of my nose
and down my throat.
When Lassie died, then the canary,
and then Gram, who'd been
my safety, I did cry!
I grew and grew, cried
myself to sleep at night.
Had children, teenagers, and cried.
The last time?
I just can't remember.
I never cried again. Now I have
dry eye syndrome and use
saltwater drops.

I Could Tell You About

Bucky, the horse I always rode.
She came from down the street,
bought for $200, a mutt horse
but she didn't know that,
came along with her name:
cute, I thought, until I rode her,
that fat little rodeo pony!
I had bruises that looked like abuse
and the saddle horn became my best friend.
That short, fat steed, smarter than I.
You couldn't put shoes on that horse.
She always needed a pedicure.
Home was her goal even before the ride
as we placed the hackamore.
She plotted while we tightened the girth.
She'd walk me into fences then laugh at me,
under branches – and she'd chuckle.
I learned her ways and she learned mine.
On the streets she'd balk at puddles, lines,
dark patches on asphalt, wouldn't move.
A stick in the hand was all she needed,
a mere twig that she could see.
She'd plod forward not laughing anymore.
The day we rode the unpaved freeway to Orcas Park
and through the stream she lay down
rolled me over, sputtering, wet,
I knew I was no horse person.
On the way home she galloped us
up the steep terraces of the 210.
What heart! What speed! Such was my last defeat.
Bucky died at a very old age
in someone else's arms
with no shoes, only her blanket
and all of her pride.

Curiosity

"Only the curious
have, if they live, a tale
worth telling at all."
~ Alastair Reid

I watch her
cut chocolate milk
with scissors,
sprinkle the stones
with kool-aid,
pour water on sand
to make it grow.
I listen as she talks
to an attentive crow,
wonder
what she knows
that I do not.
I stop her
when she climbs the fence
to peer over a precipice.

It hauled men
to the moon.
Dissected bodies
in secret.
Saw bats and frogs
inside a hollow tree.
Curiosity, that fuel
that feeds the hot fire.

I lay out the cards
again and again
to see if they will play
the same way twice.

Television

Her eyes tell me she is lost
in that cartoon world
where dead men rise
to laugh and run,
where dirt doesn't spoil your clothes,
tasks are left undone
with no consequence.
In ten minutes the world is well.
The wacky wizard is not bad, but good.
The end is just the beginning.
The end, for Barbie, who never sweats
to drive by in a car that never breaks,
where the sun is always shining.
I blank the screen into this world.
She comes home to me. Slowly.

Night Lights

Like a cat lapping at the window
is the darkness —
a small sound, a tongue
letting in the night through glass.

Grandmother's bedroom
held a safe glow for sleeping alone,
not too bright to chase away my dreams,
yet fierce enough to scare monsters
hiding under the bed.

Bright enough to make a seam
around the blackout shades
shielding the feverish room
where my mother tended me.
In shadows sickness spread
from blanket to floor.
That light — too small inside,
too bright outside to please
the air raid warden as he passed by.

Tonight, a twenty-five watt bulb guards
night wanderers from ditches,
from crooked paving stones, swaying walls.
It keeps the earthquakes away, yes
as a flashlight will do, from that room
which shook so hard in January, 1994.

Outside, a thin moon shines vaguely,
a question mark surprised by darkness.
Too dark to save the wanderer
who stepped into the wall,
while the cat slept.
Too much light.
Not enough.

PORTRAITS

Pages

Dappled light and pure darkness
cover the pages of my childhood.
Only the brightest moments stay
like a black and white photo,
moments frozen, captured,
remembered, like
my mother when she drove past me,
leaving me to walk home.
Shadowy, transparent
are the times she spent with me;
warm camphor oil stroked
on my sick, stuffy chest,
then lunch arranged on a tray,
a flower, a glass of ginger ale.
She read Black Beauty to me
all the way through
while I tried so hard to breathe.
There was that terrible night
before my surgery
when she lay on the bed beside me
cramped, exhausted, through night hours.
I forgive her for teaching fear to me,
that all men are bad, that
no one can be trusted.
I love her for her white, balled hands
when she taught me how to drive.
There should be more dappled moments.
I should be able to see through the dark.
But that is all. There are only blank pages
in the rest of the book.

Lessons

I watched my mother as I grew,
learned to be a woman.

When Mama was fifty she showed me
how it is to be a widow and alone.

She showed me sixty.
I saw how she did it.

When she was seventy
I began to follow.

Soon my mother will teach me
how to be eighty

and I am afraid.

*My mother did teach me to be eighty, ninety,
then ninety-two.*

I was right to be afraid.

Women's Wear

In the heavy winter coat
I am a winter woman
with skis and skates
beside me.
The wind blows, the sun
beats down to find
the shed cloak lying on the grass.
Beneath winter are
shorts and tennis shoes.
Then I am summer,
a swimmer in a swim suit.
Wrapped in a robe
I am a sweet night woman.
I always know what I am
by the clothes I put on,
by the shed lives, by
the pulled-on garments.
I have not yet met
the autumn woman, nor
have seen what she may wear.

Cycles

I can't do much about it
with the moon pulling and all.
The tide flows in, and out
of my eyes pours water.
This craziness. First damming
up my cells, then flowing,
and my thirst catching up.
Oh God! Under the crest
of this wave I fall,
sea water and sand in every fold,
my sandpaper skin a threat
to the tender faces of children.
Dirty and clean at once,
foaming to a fresh-water-fall
over my hair, then
a deep sweet pool. I run
free to chase the moon
before it hides its face.
Before the light comes only
from galaxies.

Well, then, and how was *your* day?

By evening, my head, so full, had burst.
Morning had brought on a clogged drain and rain,
afternoon, a meeting with too many words, black birds,
all of them careening to cause an explosion
and a blackout on my part. In my heart.
Supper was ruined and I rejected myself
calling myself incompetent, inferior, invalid, alid.
By evening I had erased myself from the list
of useful humans, bathed my body, then collapsed, elapsed,
shattered and broken forever, ever.

A Found Poem

The Lists

copy – bug bomb – bank
hair-do – blow dry – cut
write a note to thank
make the window shut
gift for Ginger – something nice
be sure there's Trisha's tray of ice
pick up girls at two diff schools
sure to chlorinate the pool
call the dentist and the doc
get a battery for the clock
make a salad for the brunch
golly 30 is a bunch!
Bring apples, pretzels, seedless grapes
to the hall by half-past 8
sew the buttons on his shirt
sweep outside. So much dirt!
Pick up book, order cakes
how many meetings will it take
to drive me crazy over the edge
oh yes, yes, buy a can of Pledge

A Song of Myself

I sing of myself a song
to sing for myself.
I come from winter's cold ice
into the scald of summer sun
melting into September.

A barcode is that which I am;
48-549-2974 - 5'4", many stone,
818 951 1041, 6 23 36
3 MTY 119, ACMC 4395
A password, a code, an http,
sassycat.com.
I loaf and invite my soul
atoms upon atoms,
space upon space,
time upon time – relative to...
My memory is a shallow grave
for numbers I cannot cipher
and letters: DJ, PTA, LLHS, GHS...
A victim of all who lived before me,
a child of my own experience.
Letters wrap around me to define
an M, an H, S and T, CA.
If my hair was bright red
and if my numbers dropped away
and if the alphabet was broken,
would you know me?
If you have a touch-tone phone,
please, leave a message. I will
return your call as soon as possible.

Tell Me a Story

What can I tell you when you ask again?
Only the known? Or my guarded secrets?
"Tell me a story" no longer means to you
some nursery rhymes and fables,
but my private memories and my lessons.
Shall I tell you about the suicide,
the one on Devil's Hill?
The boys rode up the steep hill on old Bucky,
rode down fast to say there was a man in a car.
The other said, "and the motor's running."
Dad rode up and saw the hose on the exhaust,
opened the door and felt for pulse.
Empty whiskey bottles piled up on the floor,
paperback books littered all space,
the dead man sat on the front seat floor,
his head on the passenger seat.
A helicopter flew over. "Hey," the boys said,
"maybe we'll be on TV!"
The police officer replied, "No." He said,
"this happens every day, this isn't news."

I could tell you about our first kisses, Grampa and I.
We didn't know how to do it. We learned easily.
And kept practicing so we wouldn't forget.
I have photos of the proms: he in a suit and I
wrapped in layers of tulle. Or the pigeons, I could tell
how a white one arrived when your mother was born.
I could tell how it wouldn't leave, roosting
on our Renault Cavalier convertible. Your Dad
took it up to the park and let it fly away.
The day your uncle was born a bird perched
above the porch. It was brown.
We learned that pigeons brought babies.

Imagine our thoughts when a black pigeon
flew desperately, trapped in the garage
and we wondered whose baby that would be.

I could tell you about all the relatives, the feisty farm folk,
the lovely grandmothers I knew, the struggles.
Perhaps now I'll just tell you about the treasure hunts.
You made one for me and I hunted, followed the clues,
studied the map, finally to find my treasure, and how
I loved it.
It was a demitasse cup with no saucer borrowed from my
little box, the one that held my memories.

I Could Tell You

about my Grampa, Edward James,
an orphan who grew up with cousins.
I heard he was a very bad boy
and an undependable husband.

At my Dad's drug store
Grampa cashiered at the cigarette bar,
at the liquor corner, for candy bars.
He saved a bit out here and there
when cigarettes and sugar were rationed.
Embarrassing, he was, with bad language,
a rough man with a Santa Claus belly,
a chain smoker who left cigarette stains
on every surface and smoke rings in the air.
In the morning he let me help him
burn the trash. Once, he allowed me to
light the fire. It blazed hot with all that paper,
all that cardboard, all those boxes.
My face was hot with fire and joy.
I looked up into the hillside to see
other ribbons of smoke rising into
the clear morning air.
The moment had come for a small girl
to see evidence of a larger world,
as neighbors, too, burned
their waste in the morning,
all turned to ash.

Grampa had a black sedan, 1935 model
with tiny windows in the back.
He couldn't see back or sides, it didn't matter,
the car knew where it was when it
bumped to a stop.

There are still iron rails
put in the alley by my Dad
to protect the gas meter and the plaster walls,
from Leapin' Lena, Grampa's car,
even now, these sixty-more years later.
The black devil sedan ran over
cans and curbs, toys, maybe boys.

Just one more secret and now we all know it:
Gram's pies, just baked for the meeting
of the Friendship Circle disappeared during the night
because HE ATE Them! Grampa, a man
among men, a woman's cross to bear.

MARRIAGES

Mates for Life

Two birds fly wing to wing
in sky ravaged by dying sun
to find the place
where the day ends and night begins
wing to wing they glide
then soar and dive
whirl in twilight wind
hungry they hunt
heavy they descend
in faith for the last mouse
who stays out too long
shoulder to shoulder
orange-tipped wings
cross the boundary
then fly home content
for they did not disturb
Destiny.

Old Marriage I

I see you strong, leading me.
You are close to the sun
while I look upon the moon.
Are your enduring ways
born of might, my love?
Or of the quiet of desperation?
Come, let me love you.
Rest, sit beside me,
put your strength aside.
My moonbeams fall upon us now.
My touch is soft upon your hair.
Tomorrow is soon enough
to be strong.

Old Marriage II

The taste of you my love is...
salty through these tears
and bitter as tree olives.
The taste of you, my love
sweet, too, as sweet
as jelly candy
with a lemon chaser.
You are a question stew,
my love, but rich as you are,
as quaint and inedible,
I still need nourishing;
salad and bread,
a piece of apple pie.

Old Marriage III

How happy you are, my dear,
in mid-life re-nesting:
painting window edges with
no masking, planting
fifteen patio plants
which hang frail
in the summer sun.
How proud you are
of your gifts.
Accepting, I scrape edges,
water twice a day, not knowing
how to tell you that now
you make ever stronger
the bars of my prison.

Old Marriage IV

I see you
lying on the sofa
basted with
the blue light
of after-hours
programming,
your face
ghost-pale
in sleep.
I napped
on the water bed
from ten to two
cold and blue
in a puddle
of street light.
Where have you been
my Romeo?
Am I forgotten?
I have no vial
no potion for love.
Come, stumble
away with me
to another new day
and the script
of a hurried kiss
in morning rush.

Old Marriage V

In the deep, fearful darkness of night
I lie beside you waiting for dawn.
I ache. I am afraid.
I touch you as you turn and I say
sleep well.
Morning comes with bright light
shooting through the window
dazzling the curtains.
You smile, touch my face.
I am safe.

Love Mended

That old threadbare word – love
flows in a fabric patterned
with shades of crimson colors,
whispers of mauve and the yellow of dry sun.
Chopin wove love into the air,
Monet stroked it onto canvas.

That word so often patched
nearly falls apart, its meaning frayed –
until a newborn cries
or a daughter becomes a bride,
until the lace of fifty years together
fully knits. Love unravels
until a friend perceives and cherishes,
until there is an ear ready to listen,
a shoulder to cry on. Love is repaired
with the consecration of all the threads.

Then, there is delight in love's stitching,
the worn word renewed
into the One Love.
Mended.

NEIGHBORS

The Migrant

My name is Mario, he said,
nodding a downhead nod,
murmuring in a language
English-not-English,
Spanish-not-Spanish.
Their smiles stay fixed,
afraid to retract,
teeth drying.
Honesty could threaten
if written on
unposed faces.

Buenos tardes, she said,
early in the morning.
She trembles now.
He trembles, too.

Behind her fixed face
she thinks of the law.
She remembers
her son's college friend
who needs a job.
She worries about
"the right thing."

Behind his smile
Mario thinks about his life —
one more meal,
one more night of shelter,
just one chance.

Her jungled yard
stands ugly before them.

Her terrible back
still aches
from picking weeds.
Unpaid bills remind her
the college boy charges
more than double.

She pays him with dollars
wrapped in guilt.
He comes again.
And again.

Day Laborer

She thinks she hears his cry.
She thinks she knows his pain.
She thinks he came from
Bushes and dirt
In the center of desert.
She thinks he grew up small
On one tortilla a day.

She does not know. No,
She does know
That she will never understand.
His voice blends with her garden.
She listens with her tin ear.
Spring grasses, red-apple cuttings,
The beauty of the hillsides
Gives to both of them
A little song, and
They sing it together,
Understanding not each other,
But the lovely moment.

I Wonder If I Will
Ever See John Again

I knew John pretty well,
John who lived in the weeds,
who slept on a mattress
inside a blanket in a small
hollowed space
sheltered by field oats
and an oak tree.
John went away north one day,
said, "Good bye, I'm leaving."
Now I know Margaret
who lives in the same weeds,
John's weeds,
rests beneath the same tree
in the center of John's garden.
His Rudolph the Reindeer
pyracantha will glow
this Christmas
just as John planned
with red, red berries
right on its nose.
John's hand-swept walkway
is now Margaret's sitting place.
She nibbles on nasturtiums
while she looks far away
into that place where she is,
waits. Morning comes,
then night, again and again.
If John comes back
will there be room enough
for two?

Dead Man

Blistering heat.
Hot sand, boulders,
dry chaparral; a slow walk
in heavy heat.
Snakes hide,
lizards do push-ups on rocks.
Curious boys wander by.

They thought he was dead, the man
who looked like a bundle
under the bushes,
not like the usual drunk
or a homeless man asleep in the shade,
that man in a suit, dark blue,
a shirt, white, and a red tie.
With a stick they nudged him.
Hot sand, boulders,
dry chaparral; a slow look
as thin breath came out with a sigh.
The shock of it, so much death
from the large man-body
in the Big Tujunga Wash.
The boys poured water on his face
emptying the canteen, water that rolled off
into the grains of sand and was gone.
The dead man breathed, nothing else.
They said, like on TV,
"Are you all right?" and "Check for bleeding."
No one touched, no one wanted to do
mouth-to-mouth.
One bluebelly sat wisely
making no decision.

Someone ran home, called 911.
An ambulance shook up the trail, siren blasting,
lurched on top of 200 feet of alluvium,
toward a yell, "Over here!"
One police car came.
The poor guy moved.
They went to work on him, took him away.
The finders never got his story.

The next week, in the *Foothill Leader*
the report said, "Man Found in Tujunga Wash.
Pronounced dead on arrival
at Verdugo Hills Hospital."

Jury Duty

The Census, from the window,
Sixth and Commonwealth, Los Angeles

lawyers, black suits
carts full of cases
black BMWs
young boys
trudge slow
wear heavy jackets
black, and
ski caps. It's cold.
Only 9 SUVs in the lot
not like La Canada.
Winter trees look lonely.
The accused
dress like Sunday,
jurors in jeans and shirts.
Seven trucks, 25 sedans.
Polyester stirrup pants,
umbrellas.
The Hollywood sign
across the valley
shows me where we are
this day, this long day,
among judicial personnel
uniformed in black.
Somewhere below,
buried deep
the ones before us
from 1700 AD
dressed in furred cloaks
carry hides and pouches of tallow.

They fade into a tattered,
dirty flag, stars melting into stripes,
in the church yard
across from the Superior Court
of the Pueblo de Nuestra
Senora de la Reina de Los Angeles.
On a telephone wire
hangs an empty plastic bag.

Mother

She was laden, no other word for it,
pushing the stroller on the gravel road,
holding the second grader's hand.

But not just that; a half-gallon milk jug
hung above the left wheel,
a bag of briquettes perched
on the top, the infant asleep
on a pillow, and all uphill.

If only she'd had the car this day
to better plan the barbecue
for the Fourth of July.
Red, white, blue streamers
and the flag on the neighbor's garage
couldn't give her that second wind.

With legs aching, heat flowing out of her
she almost lost patience, almost grabbed
a switch for Jennifer. *Please, Jen,*
just a few more steps.

Inside the gate, relief rose
and blossomed
like the sage flowers
in her garden,
standing straight up and blue.

Pity Party - Conversations with Me and Dee

I know it's cold so far in the north
but it's cold here, too, that's the truth!
It's so cold the troughs freeze over,
the cattle are thirsty, the field is snow-covered.
Cold is cold, cousin Dee;
there, it's C something,
by gosh, here. It's 43 F.
Poor you, poor me.
We have heat in summer
rattlers and slugs, I know,
you have heat and mosquito bugs.
We work so hard all day in the fields,
worry at night 'bout 10% yields!
Well, think of us,
two hours to commute.
I shouldn't compare, but
snow piles up to 6 feet high!
Gets so hot our lake fish fry!
Hails so hard it dents our cars!
Smog's so bad we can't see stars!
Blows so hard dust covers home!
Ground splits open
when earthquake comes!
Locust come, geese eat the grain!
We get floods after rains!
Cows hit cars on country roads!
Semis buckle and spill their loads!
Shopping malls are far away!
Crowds down here waste the days!
Poor you, it's true, and
poor me, cousin Dee.

Pen Pals

I read your letter once more,
the past seems sweet now, looking back
as nostalgia creeps like hot chocolate
over ice cream.
You reminded me
of those times:
we rode our ponies uphill
until we fell off backward,
drove Dad's truck into the river
where it floundered in mud.
You were always in trouble. I laugh.
Your memories here in this letter,
such good stories.
Inside me I feel afraid, sad
at the remembering.
Paper, envelope, stamp,
pen at my fingertips to return
that life to you, make friends
with our childhood.
Your letter lies open and read.
This paper stays beneath my hand,
my pen gone dry.

SEASONS

Everywhere

water drops in a London flat
a canary sings in Paris
scree falls in Utah
falls on a silenced beetle
just one B-flat howls in Sylmar
the intruder is caught
a stone scims on Lake Victoria
close to shore
thrown by a boy called Skip

water drops from a faucet in a London flat
everywhere there is movement
please that it shall never stop
a traveler, lonely, lodges with strangers
wind blows steady across the plains
Canada, the Ukraine
the first golden leaf falls
on still water
one pomegranate tree stands fruited with crows
rice paddies shine in moonlight
voices sing out camp songs in the tour bus

rain falls drop by drop on Paris fires
a tall man removes his tie in a Singapore hotel
a hungry woman eats hamster from a Beijing vendor
garlic fields are ready for harvest in Gilroy
a virus mutates in Gabon
a ball is thrown through a window
where there is no glass

water drips in a London flat
in Oz the wizard roars hiding the sound

of footfalls in the dark
water falls gently in a Tokyo garden
rice steams in a bamboo pot
while a family breathes out breath
across the universe of ocean
to Ellis Island and the Pacific
in view of Liberty
on the Island of Manhattan
a whinny, a hoofbeat, the call of fowl
from a dusty yard

water drips from a well bucket
red dust flies
at the Baptist mission in Coimbatore
sea anemones open their mouths on Tahiti shores
ma-ma-ma cries all over the world
the rector prays in a soft voice
mothers sing softly their lullabies
an echo from the cathedral choir
rises into treetops, disappears
ice rattles in goblets
dice crack against table sides
wine spills on a white cloth
as the ship rolls side to side

water drips in a London flat
"gone" – say the nurses
a clock chimes
water pours to cleanse hands
white sand blows away
from Tasmanian shore
hot springs bubble in Iceland
newborn kittens cry feebly
a puma runt in a large litter

snow geese call, leave a wake of wings
flames roar in Paris

water drips in a London flat
a luncheon outside is serenaded
by the whisper of wasp wings
one dead leaf falls in a Zen garden
on pure white sand
autumn bellows in Vermont
reds and yellows and browns
feasts for eyes, blankets for seeds
water drips in a London flat

while we sleep.

A Tale to Tell

They built a house
with no understanding,
straw with no plaster.
They built a house
with no understanding,
with warped boards
and bent nails,
stones with no mortar,
on *no* foundation.
The house built
upon sand.

The people were afraid of nothing,
not even the huff and puff
of the big bad wolf.
They slept deep and
in peace.
Until that morning
when the big bad wolf
turned on the rumbling,
shaking of the earth below.
Shelters upended,
pipes hung loose,
wires tangled in mid-air.
the people were bewildered.
Someone said, "We need
to fix this." First,
a foundation,
deep.

Mother's Day

Mint leaves from her garden,
baby carrots, snap peas,
red-ripe tomatoes and apricots...
As with paint pots before canvas
and her hands the brushes,
she arranges the color of the meal.
Monet's gardens stay for centuries,
hers are devoured in an hour,
live only in memory. Meals:
potatoes sprinkled with parsley,
lamb with Asian pear and kiwi salsa,
chipotle glazed apples,
chicken orecchiette soup
with lemon grass and cilantro,
vanilla bean soufflés,
flour pudding, corn pones
with butter and syrup.
Her hands fashion
bok choy cooked crisp-tender,
haggis and ale, oatcakes and mutton.
A treat of strawberry ice cream,
grilled cheese, chocolate milk.
Mother.
Warm bread, the morning's cream,
corn cob jelly, French toast.
Acorn mush, piki, and a sprig of sage.
The maker of fine art.
My mother.

Easter Sunday

That Easter, Sunday,
the year 1923, the hour 4:30
on that clear, cold morning,
trumpet song flared wide
into the rays of the rising sun
calling one and all to the hillside cross.
A damp trail led upward,
a pilgrimage path,
rocky, slippery in places
on Easter Sunday.
They walked on singing,
their voices poured magic
wide across the valley.
That day, the people gathered.
Father Tonelli raised his hands in blessing.
The Baptist choir sang,
every kind of believer stood
beneath the cross
named for San Ysidro,
Patron Saint of Little Homes.
The Love was there too,
dropped in for a bit.

No Grapes This Year

There are no grapes this year, my dear,
so we will make wine with beets,
drink it down with a flourish,
a rousing toast.
And this year the cotton is dry.
The corn is as high as an elephant's eye
but the cobs are bare.
This is not a good year, my dear.
The Big Tujunga River
flows with rock and sand,
rattlers scream in that hot sun,
lizard lines lie wavy on sand,
all the rodents hide away.
The evening, when canyon breeze blows,
seems kinder. Deer feed.
Crows cry out, wrens warble good-nights,
It was on such a late afternoon
where, beneath rock and sand,
dead center of the riverbed
we found forks and spoons,
a baby blanket well used,
and a medal with its two words:
To Joe. We took them all home,
rescued them, gave them
a tender place to stay.
As the shadows stretched long
the Big Tujunga, with its boulders
bathed in last light,
accepted darkness.

Autumn, 1950

It was ninety degrees
those two days and nights
when hot desert winds
blew steady through the valley.

Hot desert winds blow
steady through the valley
hour after hour
pushing down trees
flipping roofs from walls
of homes once thought
fortresses
against natural disaster
and the anger of gods.
Two days. Two nights
hot winds blow.
There is no light in the night,
spiral stove burners
stay cold and nobody
eats cooked meat,
wood fire flame
would blow with the wind.
Breath still breathing is stolen,
sucked away to wet such dryness.
Flashlights light bedtime faces
but sleep stays away, walled out
by howls, by crashing of objects
once admired.
Manicured streets,
once-perfect gardens
hold the crops, fruit
ripped away by malicious hunger

wasted on hungry wind,
while charred branches
from a sparked fire
scatter themselves helplessly
in ravines. Old trees,
no longer majestic,
lay face down and dying, worn out.
Small boulders litter the highway,
shoved, rolled through the night.
It is fearsome
when hot desert winds
blow steady through the valley.

Station Fire

One morning

In my dream I sat beside a campfire
like the one at the lakes,
waiting for the scent of coffee.
Strange, the dream had curtains
and a closet door.

That terrifying day
our eyes opened to yellowed walls.
Outside, the dawn world
was rising orange.
Outside, smoke and ash
would burn our noses and fall lightly
over every object.
Inside, outside, that ash
would congeal, become
like cement, hard to wash away.
The fire had begun to consume.
It grew and could not be stopped.
Yes, we fear and despise this fiery world,
yet we still sleep and feast,
sew and read beside our windows, living
in the path of what, we hope, will not happen.
We pretend that fire is obsolete.
My father once tried to calm my fears:
Volcanoes and earthquakes, floods and fires
will never happen again.
But they do, the disaster is waiting.
So we delight ourselves, right now,
at this early hour of the morning,
with the black and orange world advancing.
We are safe, for the moment.

Wild Fire

Simi, Moorpark, Val Verde, Fillmore, Piru
Waterman, Arrowhead, Cedar Glen, Crestline,
Hemet, Malibu, San Diego County, Julian,
The Old Fire, Grand Prix Fire, Cucamonga,
Paradise, Twin Lakes, Running Springs,
Devore, Highland, Stevenson Ranch,
Valencia, Porter Ranch...
burn and burn again:
Clear is the red inside my eyes
and black the blankness of deep night,
the awakening to another orange morning,
another ochre sky. On the shelf,
the complete works of Will Durant and
"Good Night Moon" below the lamp.
Dry winds have come to light the fires,
to destroy the clearness of the mountains.
Ra, The Sun, blew His hot breath,
dried the face of the world,
then lit it to see his own image.
I lift my hands to feel the rain
of ashes, touch my hair to feel embers.
On the windowsill, a tomato,
a persimmon, home-grown.

What Would This Mean?

What if,
beneath this laden table
where heads bow in gratitude,
berries pile in a cut-glass bowl,
asparagus and fresh corn steam,
what if,
beneath this table of wiggling children
and great-grandma's folded hands,
under our feet, below the wood and slab,
there would be hardened prints
of warriors?
Pieces of rusted knives,
black arrowheads,
a lost flintlock
in a place where men fought,
left blood, and lives, to lie?
What would be the purpose of the prayer?
Or the wars?
Or the generations of family
just lifting their forks?

A Terrible Awful No Darn Good Day

It was that kind of a day
when sleep gathers in
the corners of eyes
and they sting, when
clouds hang low and
rain splatters the dusty car,
the kind of day that is
full of webs and spiders
and all things that suck and
sting, and you feel
juicy and succulent,
when the temperature is
137 degrees in the shade,
the roof has caved in and
the wind has
whipped up a forest fire.
That no darn good day you
slice up a supper of cucumbers
and sauerkraut, then
cry yourself to sleep, and your
dream world closes in to a
garbage pail just
like the real world,
and everything blows up
and *you* have to shovel up the mess.
However,
the rain poured down hard and
washed the spiders out.
Then, the clouds blew away
and the sun came out,
and dried up
all the rain.

What Am I Thankful For?

Why, for this little seed
caught between my teeth!
This seed from berries
cooked into jam
mounded in the cut-glass dish
my mother gave to me,
sweet jam boiled
from my own berries
piled on bread
bought from Ralph's
just two blocks away,
bread made from flour
ground from grain
grown on great fields,
grain that drank rain
dropped from clouds
that were coaxed from the sea,
grain, fed by the sun
that hangs in the great galaxy
spinning the universe,
which hangs above this sweet earth
while it turns over and over,
where, under gathered clouds
heavy with rain
coaxed from the sea
which wakens the soil
rich with grain,
ripened kernels of wheat,
are milled into flour
to be baked into bread
which I can buy at Ralph's
just two blocks from here

on which I can spread
this mound of jam
resting in the cut-glass dish
my mother gave me,
sweet jam made from my own berries
whose little seed
is caught between my teeth.

Slippingsliding

The days of
Christmastime
edge together
twisting, bending
forming a ribbon
ribboning
into a pathway
slick with
dewdrops and
gasoline and I
stumble and
slide out of
control
losing my
balance, rushing
downhill. As the
pathway slopes
steeply I reach out
to clutch at
dark spots called
night. These
Christmas days are
sliding, sliding
toward boxes
and ribbons
food and light;
sliding, sliding
down toward
One Wondrous Day.
Please, this time
may I not
crash past the
moment, fall off

the side, pass
through time
find myself
slipping too far
missing the knowing
losing the feeling
of sliding, sliding
on toward
Love.

SMALL THINGS

Work of the Hands

Shear, card, spin, fashion the thread,
knit, purl, stitch, needles click
in and out thread under, over,
then shirred, embellished
into a garment as fine as fine art.
Hand, eyes, colored yarns,
all that is needed for soft warmth,
for coverings, for beauty.
Under the light of a single lamp
socks are knit for the boys,
a sweater for little sister, mittens
for the baby, lace tatted for
a trousseau.
Once my grandma fixed a hole in my sock,
put down a hem in my favorite dress,
made a tiny dress for my baby.
These garments, created
stitch by stitch, lie in the cedar chest
ready for new children.

Three of Hearts

My mother's tablecloth,
hand-crocheted over years
is a true work of art.
Covered with clear plastic
it decorates the dining room table
which is used for papers
and books and tableaus and dining.
I lay out on it the old cards,
the ones she bought for me
at the Calgary airport;
rough-edge tributes
to my nervous hands
for solitaire.
On my mother's plastic covered
artistry, built stitch by stitch,
I build stacks of numbers,
just as we used to do together, she
supervising.
Ones and twos on aces,
and a queen which covers a king
and when the sequence is complete
I swipe it away, the evidence
of accomplishment
which has no real meaning. I do it
again and again. I depend this time
on one three of hearts
which does not appear.

Spring Cleaning

What do I need with this jar of broken flowers?
Why did my grandmother dry them,
place them in this bit of glass, keep them?
The last to touch them was Nella Frances,
born 1887, died too soon of ovarian cancer.
Do you suspect, as I do, that she had a lover?
Did the two of them hide in a field somewhere,
pluck wild flowers? Kiss?
Were these petals handed to her by *him?*
What will I miss by letting them leave me?
My Gram, I loved her.
These dead flowers, last touched
by my father's mother,
soon will be touched by me.
They will hold us to each other.

The Decorator from Penny's

entered.
She placed a smile on her face which showed her teeth,
the "O Dahling!" smile. I saw her dread
of this granny house, this grampa home.
I understand a condescending attitude. I recognize
an "O must I" droop. I see her eyes
eliminate
Sister's floral porcelains, the lamp from Italy,
Grampa's floor clock and his refinished propeller.
She'll tell us we'll have space if we
eliminate
the beat up piano still gouged
from the earthquake tumble.
She'll rid us
of Grandmother's painting of roses, the cut glass
my mother used and all her tea time treasures.
Photographs. Everywhere. Of everyone. At all ages.
She sees the terrible patchy fading of the rug,
mauve, against light green drapes.
We sit, drink a cup of tea. She takes out samples.
I have an epiphany. I give them back
and with empathy
relieve her of her job.

Right and Wrong

Your clothes are interesting, she said,
and I smiled, said "interesting"
is a long word.
Her eyes dropped to my Easy Spirits,
the scuffs and cracks there for reasons,
and I wore them with a summer dress.
As she looked away, nothing to say,
I saw myself as through her eyes:
hair rumpled by a three-year-old
with her favorite barrette on one side,
a bunny sticker on my shirt, and sand
in my pockets. My blouse, so badly used,
undone, and to my shame, missing
a button, that blouse mailed years ago,
chosen from a catalogue, on sale.
Sometimes I forget the real world,
place the nation of child's fantasy
quite in the wrong country, yet,
such a fine countryside it is.
For a moment, the stranger seemed
ridiculous. As did I.

Photograph

The Santa Anas cleared the sky
with two nights of blowing.

Wondrous light defines,
cuts lines, makes shadows.

Trees glisten mica-like,
with splashed light.

The camera snaps up
daffodils, green hills,

mountain tops and fields of poppies,
tastes a fencepost

leaning against the sky.
An old yellow ribbon hangs limp

from a winter tree.
The shutter gulps.

Zoom lens stretches
to capture this perfect moment.

In a few days, a photograph
will show a flower, some sky,

a piece of wood, a brown twisted cloth,
snapped, bathed in fluids,

traded for coin, all in a frantic effort
to keep that one miraculous day.

Broken...

...shards hidden, of a water vessel
seen one morning centuries later,
the dig a success,

crystal, the wedding set.
As the earth shook,
glass breaking against glass,

like a young heart
at its loss of first love,
tendrils of affection falling away.

My mother's beloved cup,
from her grandma,
kept on the highest shelf
away from small hands.

With miniature toys inside,
so coveted by a child
who had learned how to climb.

Great grandmother's cup,
pieces strewn on the kitchen floor.
After sixty years –
still un-forgiven.

Broken, breaking, shattering
straight into the trash bin,
the city dump. Someday
to be exalted by a college class
at a successful dig.

All That I Am

All those small murders!
Could it be that each life
passes into the killer's hands
like the souls of warriors
at a cannibal feast?
Will I pay for all those last breaths
as they passed from an ant,
from a bee, and a cricket,
as they changed molecules
into my beating soul?
Then I am a trail of ants,
I am houseflies and moths,
vipers and centipedes.
The heaviness of this burden!
Then I must also be
rats in the attic, mold in the cellar.
The bellowing steer,
Carrots pulled
from their moist brown home.
The cremated sycamore tree?
Did I breathe this in, too?
If so, I am all that I am
and much, much more.

Silence

Ther6e is something about
silence...its weight,
the way it inhales,
leaves the room clear
for thought.
Though quiet is never pure
as all the world knows.
Take away the whirr of fans,
traffic's drone,
and leave the sky
clear and quiet.
Turn the voices off,
quiet the old record.
Sound still creeps in
with the call of birds,
scrambled scree
on the hillside,
bees, or a night
full of crickets.
Without these,
the beating sound
of one's own heart.
One evening
we sat moon-bathing,
listening for nothing.
But the silence,
so light, so fragile,
just slipped away.

The Small Things

It's those small things that make a memory
like my Granny winding her hair on a crooked pin
for the night and then placing broom straws
in her earlobes to keep her earring holes open.
My other Grandma put her finger in her nose,
saw me watching and said, don't do this,
your nose will be as big as mine.
Corri winds her hair around her finger when she
is thinking and Trisha swings her foot.
My mother straightens all she sees.
My father's comfort food was flour and milk,
brought to a boil, covered with cream, brown sugar,
nutmeg. Sometimes saltines crushed in milk.
I know someone who eats French toast with ketchup.
I still keep the cream pitcher that Gramps used in his
room behind the store. These are the small things
that bring my people back to me.

PASSAGES

Time

Time measures itself
in layers of dust
hidden behind books
and on windowsills
where it sleeps, unnoticed
for many months.

Time cannot be brushed away.
It cherishes confusion.
It changes the faces of children,
whitens up the hair.
Then it yawns
and curls into a ball,
on the sofa, watching flames
in the fireplace.

Things, unseen
for many months,
shift and disappear.

There is a clock in this box;
pictures of us since our time
began. What need is there
for other proof?

Time Capsule from 1914

Shovelful by shovelful, they hack
through hard-packed ground.
Rock and pebble cascade
into a summer-dry hole
until the chink of metal on wood
promises that time is returned,
bound in a watertight vessel,
wax and tarpaper, sealed to last.
Twelve heads bow over,
to see the messages placed there
from the past, in the capsule
of time. Open, rip, pry, twist,
the empty tube holds nothing but the title,
and 100-year-old mud:
Class of 1914 – Remember Us.
Where is my mother's baby ring,
uncle's first tooth, the grandfather's Bible?
What happened to Gwen Nelson's letter,
Percy Savage's poem, *An Ode to a Small Place?*
I see the list here in my hand, the contents
named and each line signed.
A calling card, an Indian stone,
a crucifix from the Ukraine,
a brand new dime.
Along with time itself,
its symbols have vanished,
hidden inside the mud.

West of Hillrose

In 1959 there was that donkey
who would bray when our neighbor
kissed her date good night.
Once, very late, the shaggy beast got loose,
shoved his head in our front door
where he and I stood face to face.
In mutual surprise.
Our road meandered,
dusty and curving around a hillside
accosted by lupines and spring grasses.
A chestnut colt jumped and kicked
in his field beside a pepper tree.

In 1960
a white pigeon cuddled on the porch
the day we brought our baby home,
wouldn't leave. That was the fourth of July.
An earth-colored bird moved in
to greet our newborn son two years later
on the third of July.
It was logic – pigeons bring babies.
We paid three-ninety-five that one month for gas
for our thrifty black Renault stick shift,
one hundred fifty-two dollars and seventy-one cents
for the mortgage, bought hamburger and hot dogs
on sale.
To make a home: plant, paint, plaster,
replace, rewire, repeat, re-wash,
buy light bulbs, grout, paper over cracked plaster,
water, re-seed, fertilize, trim, cut back,
buy washing machine, cereal and soap,
never run out of milk...

In 1965
late, after dark, in the corral,
the horses nickered and snorted,
a comforting sound.
Once, Lacota caught a halter strap
on the feed bin, reared, was crazed.
It was the middle of the night.

It was about 1970.
They were riding Bucky that day
up and down the hillside.
The boys said, "There's a car up there
on top of the hill, its motor's running
and there's smoke inside."
The dead man slumped amid
whiskey bottles and paperback books.
The police said, "Oh, this happens every day."

It was 1971
when the earthquake shook down the block wall,
broke the tangerine trees to the ground.
Now the blooms scent the evening.
The fruit is hard and bitter, drops too soon.
Once-in-a-while we listened
to the train on its way
to San Fernando, its horn
and a deep rumble. We counted cars
in our minds on the way to sleep.

1980, it was
when times were good we joined
the Book-of-the-Month Club
bought record albums of Harry Belafonte
at Carnegie Hall, and a good turntable.
Children played with scabbed knees,

grew many new teeth, long legs.
Our little girl wore a
gunnysack formal to graduation
and he a new suit too short at the wrists.

1993
Around the table now, four at each side,
two on each end... turkey, peas, pies, pickles,
cranberry, dressing, mashed potatoes,
prayer.
Only one baby is left to sit in the high chair.
My mother is a great-grandmother.
What a mystery! That, and the plum tree
cut down and grown again.

Take Me

Take me to the back alley of your mind
where garage doors are crooked,
gates hang askew.
Take me to the back alley doors
where trash cans overflow,
the back places where grasses
grow in honest clumps
and discarded toys list, lonely,
covered with dust and a tendril
of morning glory vine.
In the back alley of town
the grocer smokes, gets a little air.
The baker sits for a minute or more
to feel a piece of sun.
Secrets of the day
are revealed, smiled at, resolved.
Take me to that place of your home
where the back door is open,
leads into a kitchen, an honest place
of refuge. Your mother
wears slippers, an old sweater,
an apron with loose strings.
She hands you a warm crusted
slice of bread with butter
and golden syrup from a green can.
You eat it outside in the tree house
perched in a tree ready to fall
and lick syrup from your fingers.
Please, I don't want your
masked life, fancy parlor.
Take me to the back alley
of your mind.

The Alley

Where the roadway is gutted,
soil washed to center beside
unused garages too small
for an SUV,
tire tracks are deep.
Grasses grow spring-green
to hide little purple flowers;
bent-grass grows,
oats begin to form.
Back gates fall from hinges,
grey-board fences lean
on dead timbers.
A child's dump truck
lists beside a doorway,
its load of dirt eroded
by last winter's rains.
Grandfather's chicken coop
stands empty and splintered,
its black-brown boards
stained by rusty nails.
In this back alley
forgotten things fall down.
Here I wait for you,
the one I love,
and your embrace.

I Can Hear the Plodding of Beetles

I have heard of silence
deep enough to hurt the ear,
of quiet strong enough to know
the sound of blood rushing
through one's own body.
There was once in this valley
quiet enough
to made public a whisper.
Murmured conversation
pushed away miles with silence.
At night, owl called. Coyote
sang her blessing over a meal.
From a dusty trail, once,
hooves made rhythm
for a wagon's wheels,
a duet that entertained mid day.
The old parson sang
"Lord, I'm Comin' Home"
and the song was heard
clear to the hills and beyond.
The men, tired, dusty, hot,
slept outside on their cots.
Their lullabies – the cough of a friend
from across the valley, a quiet song
sung in a tent, a murmur.

Years have passed. Since then,
new sounds fill the air.
Jays still squabble,
small creatures scurry
breaking branches,
avalanching piles of pebbles.

But now, so many years present,
is a deafness from new noise.
Hammers tap duets with hand saw,
A cement truck
pounds on the ready soil,
covering the death cry
of the horned spine flower.
Roaring, as relentless as waterfall,
cascades from the freeway.
Big-rigs speed. Families rush,
the weary hurry to quieter shores.
Over a rocky place
below the asphalt of the 210
empty flatbeds thump,
bounce over that stubborn place
where tough globs of granite
lay miles deep
and three inches too high.
This morning, inside the loudness,
I see a cat's mouth
meowing a silent cry
that forms from my memory.
Heard only in my mind
is the call of mourning dove
and the sigh of breeze.
In my thoughts
I can hear the plodding of beetles.

The Remembering

She says she remembers
the dark meat of grouse
chunky with bites of buckshot,
cabbage fried in bacon grease,
one pot of potatoes for eleven children.

He says he remembers
sugared tomatoes stewed in the warm kitchen,
flour-and-milk pudding on a snowy day
with brown sugar and nutmeg.
The days they salted the pork.

She remembers
the root cellar full of salamanders,
chickens and peas and jams in jars,
muddy prints on the scrubbed floor,
hot water on the side of the stove.

He remembers
digging the well. Twilight harvests.
Piling manure on the side of the house,
ferrets in the henhouse,
the cow that nearly gored his mother.

She remembers
the one tin dipper in the wooden water bucket,
the babies coming one after the other,
the grandmother, the hired hands,
Sunday dinners, so many pies.

He says he remembers
the day they brought the Rumley home,

the joy of an easier days' work,
the calving, the horse with colic,
the Northern Lights.

She says she remembers the story
of her father coming home
over unmarked prairie,
the horses leading through blizzard,
the dot of lamplight in the frosted window.

He remembers the story
of the day a mother loaned blankets
to fevered, trail-weary men.
In a month children died,
throats closed, breath trapped inside.

She remembers
her first sight of the city
the day after they eloped,
the room they stayed in,
the frame garage that became their home.

He remembers
the job that took him from her,
the full, sweet moments of coming home,
their small corner drug store,
built together. The children.

They say they remember
as they hold hands,
speak about the new ways of things,
and of their old world
which has passed away.

FAREWELLS

Fields of my Childhood

Oh, why did you tug at the fields of my childhood?
Why did you come, steel and concrete?
Must every hill be leveled?
Like a cloth pulled from a full table
the scene disappears over the edge,
this scene, this field, these wildflowers,
pulled down from meadows into
a whole city, my quiet meadows,
my furred hillsides, my orchards and
vineyards, my dusty pathways.
Plaster-covered strip malls sit flat
on my once rounded hillocks,
tar and gravel fill creature homes.
Rubble lies in corners, in gutters.
The rain cannot replenish the earth.
My well is as dry as my stream bed. Why
have you tugged at the fields of my childhood?
I once played in dewed grass high as my thighs,
green as Springtime, thick and long it was,
I formed pathways in early morning
through clusters of poppies that
touched my fingertips. I ate grapes from vines,
watched coyotes do the same.
Why did you come, steel and glass?
Must every rise be leveled?
Didn't you see the meadows?

The Old Clock

As old as time. As old as *my* time
is the clock on the mantle at home;
mahogany brown, sloped sides,
its pendulum swinging with no thought of its own.
It sits on a faded pea-green footlocker,
Grandpa's, from the war,
My eyes look back at it now;
clock, box, shadows,
see time swing back and forth.
Grandma lies in my brother's room,
cancer taking her away by small bits.
Back and forth, time, predictable,
with no choice for anyone,
tick, tock, tick, tock,
one way then the other. Stop, I plead.
Its pendulum measures
whether I can stand the sound or not.
Back and forth, it subtracts the minutes
of my Grandma's life.
In one dark corner stands Death,
not even bothering to sit down,
a creature glaring,
a bandana slung loosely around his neck,
wears a Stetson, a Cowboy Death in boots,
lasso in hand to catch her.
He will own her, not I anymore.
Back and forth. It is the clock I remember,
pendulum monotonous in the night.

This Letter

I write to you from grief. Do you remember the roses?
How lovely the red ones are this time of year?
You photographed them, painted their portraits
yellow on black to look like velvet, they hang
over the mantel against the white wall, they are you.
My memory returns like Spring, of you and I and roses.
See? The old bushes still bloom!

Your books stand shoulder to shoulder, dusty, a family.
Your clothes are still in bags far back in the closet
where I left them, your cracked and empty shoes
good for nothing, the proof of the poverty of my spirit.
I remember the summer heat and you on your feet all day,
then your winter hands broken from too much water,
wounded from ice, the late night frost on your beard.

I write to you from grief, my love, and from guilt,
for the burden I lay upon your dying. I wanted only
that you should live. Guilt, too, that I am here
to see this Springtime, to smell these roses. By tomorrow
the fruit trees will rush into green. Peaches
will form for summer tasting.
Afternoons I sit alone. I sing and no one hears my voice.
Are my songs wasted? Were they?

My voice is now lost somewhere, this song
never to be heard again.
Your song is gone. Your glove still lies
on the work bench
where you left it, empty too, like the sound
of my singing, like the empty melody
heard by no one but myself.

Now my strength is frozen,
while memory returns wounded.
Yet, I hold the weapon ready to hurt the past,
with my present I can turn memory around
and upside down and inside out.
I can make it think it was something else.

I in my guilt and in my grief wave good-bye
as I return to living.
I have broken the bond that held me
in your decaying grasp. I turn away
from roses to sweet peas and poppies
early in the morning.

The Estate

Today would be Gerte's birthday,
today, the day I signed the checks
to impatient heirs,
the day the world said "goodbye,
and now you are really gone."

Once, an earthquake
celebrated February 9 while
her birthday cake shifted
from stove to counter.
The whole earth celebrated
Gerte's day.

Ninety three birthdays
brought that many parties,
for Gerte was a party girl.

Strange, no gifts
line the table today for
a frail and tiny lady
this February 9.
No party this year,
this, the first time,

no lemon cake
from Costco,
no wine for celebration.
served in paper cups.

The gifts went
to the givers
on this birthday.

While Gerte sleeps
below a bare dirt mound
with grasses straggling
at its edges.

Memories

Watching memories take place
way back in the mind's cave
reminds me of flowers
arranged in a tall red vase.
Daisies and mums, dwarfed by zinnias
rise above fern and baby's breath,
blue above, bright yellow below;
they don't look just right.
Now, yellow above, blue below,
and a touch of orange, yes,
better this way.
Like memories which change shape,
position this way and that,
real or not, stay in the mind,
those images from yesterday,
those before knowledge,
before language,
a look perhaps, a sound too strong,
combines. Loud above, soft below,
soft above, loud below.
I remember a face with large teeth
behind a happy smile I thought
pleasing, and I always
look for that face in any crowd.
I remember. It was real.
If any memory is real.

This Epitaph

I don't know what to write.
I really wanted to be
a ballerina, but my body
became top heavy, well,
heavy. Acrobatics, tap dancing
were not the best answer.
I really wanted to be a singer
and I was until my voice broke,
squeaked and shattered.
From yelling with laryngitis.
I really wanted to be
a helicopter pilot.
I would have been if
astigmatism and
near sightedness
had not been so profound.
I really wanted to be
a courier for the FBI
but they wouldn't have me.
SO.
I tried playing the autoharp.
I was good until
it was stolen.
I tried English handbells
until I suffered from
tendonitis.
I tried knitting and crocheting.
My son said his sweater
had one arm too long.
Uncle Fred's afghan
was a trapezoid.
Crocheted place mats
for my mother

turned into collars.
I just don't know
what to write here
on this very small
bronze grave marker
which I bought for myself.

Bury Me

with treasures;
a leaf from the cottonwoods
so I may take with me
the magic of trees.
Place in my grave
the seed of an oak
that I may hold heartwood
in my memory.
Put in a vessel of stones
from my beloved valley
that I will not become lost.
Leave in my hand
a feather from the road
that I may fly.
Then touch your hand
to my lips
that I may taste love
on my journey.

THE END

ABOUT THE AUTHOR

Marlene Hitt is a Los Angeles poet, writer and retired educator with local history as an avocation. She has served for many years as Archivist, Museum Director and Historian at the Bolton Hall Museum in Tujunga. She is a native Californian and a graduate of Occidental College. She also studied at CSUN, USC, UCLA, Glendale College and Trinity College, Ireland. As a member of the Chupa Rosa Writers of Sunland for nearly 30 years, she has worked with this small group of poets from whom has sprung readings at the local library, the Poet Laureate Program of Sunland-Tujunga, and the currently popular Village Poets.

Her poetry received several first place prizes in annual competitions of the Women's Club, San Fernando Valley, and many awards from the John Steven McGroarty Chapter of the California Chaparral Poets. Her work appeared in *Psychopoetica* (UK), *Chupa Rosa Diaries* of the Chupa Rosa Writers, Sunland (2001-2003), Glendale College's *Eclipse* anthologies, two Moonrise Press anthologies, *Chopin with Cherries* (2010) and *Meditations on Divine Names* (2012), and *Sometimes in the Open*, a collection of verse by California Poets Laureate. She published *Sad with Cinnamon*, *Mint Leaves*, and *Bent Grass* (all in 2001), as well as *Riddle in the Rain* with Dorothy Skiles, and a stack of chapbooks for friends and family.

Ms. Hitt, elected Woman of Achievement for year 2001, served as Poet Laureate of Sunland-Tujunga in 1999-2001, at the turn of the century. She has published several books on local history, including *Sunland-Tujunga from Village to City* (Arcadia, 2000, 2005) based on columns written for the *Foothill Leader, Glendale News Press, North Valley Reporter, Sentinel,* and *Voice of the Village* newspapers since 1998. Over the years, she taught in elementary school, worked in a pharmacy, chaired committees, tap-danced, and played English handbells, autoharp and ukulele. She dedicates her successes to her husband, Lloyd, her children and grandchildren, her biggest fans.

www.ingramcontent.com/pod-product-compliance
Lightning Source LLC
Chambersburg PA
CBHW020915090426
42736CB00008B/647